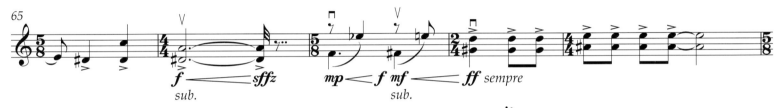

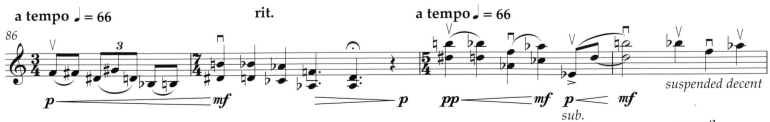

Incantation (1995) for solo violin is one of the earliest works by Augusta Read Thomas that has not been withdrawn by the composer. Her enthusiasm for the violin is exhibited in this piece and in a number of other works, including *Pulsar, Rush,* and *Caprice* for solo violin; *Spirit Musings* and *Carillon Sky* for solo violin and chamber orchestra; *Rumi Settings* for violin and cello, and *Silent Moon* for violin and viola.

The composer observes: "*Incantation* was composed for Catherine Tait, who, at the time, was dying of cancer. Tait presented the premiere performance, beautifully, shortly before her death, in a very touching recital in Rochester, NY, on 18 November 1995.

The five-minute work celebrates Tait's generosity of spirit. The music sings out, with beauty and grace, always with a richness and elegance. Falling loosely into an ABA form, it ends as it were, on a question, with a major seventh hanging in the air, unresolved."

0-73999-84661-4

0 73999 84661 4

HL50484661

G. SCHIRMER, Inc.

DISTRIBUTED BY
HAL•LEONARD®

INCANTATION
for solo violin

Augusta Read Thomas

AUGUSTA READ THOMAS

INCANTATION

FOR SOLO VIOLIN

REVISED EDITION

G. SCHIRMER, Inc.

DISTRIBUTED BY
HAL•LEONARD®